Fifth Avenue Art Galleries

Paintings in Oil and Water Colors

Fifth Avenue Art Galleries

Paintings in Oil and Water Colors

ISBN/EAN: 9783744657204

Printed in Europe, USA, Canada, Australia, Japan

Cover: Foto ©Thomas Meinert / pixelio.de

More available books at **www.hansebooks.com**

Fifth Avenue Art Galleries

366 FIFTH AVENUE

Near 34th Street

Executors' Sale

CATALOGUE

OF

Paintings

IN

Oil and Water Colors

FROM THE COLLECTIONS OF

CYRUS W. FIELD

AND

JAMES R. OSGOOD

TO BE SOLD BY AUCTION, WITHOUT RESERVE.

WEDNESDAY AND THURSDAY EVENINGS

DECEMBER 7TH AND 8TH

AT EIGHT O'CLOCK

Robert Somerville	❋	Ortgies & Co.
AUCTIONEER		MANAGERS

NEW YORK:
1892

Conditions of Sale

1. The highest Bidder to be the Buyer, and if any dispute arise between two or more Bidders, the Lot so in dispute shall be immediately put up again and re-sold.

2. The Purchasers to give their names and addresses, and to pay down a cash deposit, or the whole of the Purchase-money *if required*, in default of which the Lot or Lots so purchased to be immediately put up again and re-sold.

3. The Lots to be taken away at the Buyer's Expense and Risk upon the conclusion of the Sale, and the remainder of the Purchase-money to be absolutely paid, or otherwise settled for to the satisfaction of the Auctioneer, on or before delivery; in default of which the undersigned will not hold themselves responsible if the Lots be lost, stolen, damaged, or destroyed, but they will be left at the sole risk of the Purchaser.

4. The sale of any Article is not to be set aside on account of any error in the description. All articles are exposed for Public Exhibition one or more days, and are sold just as they are, without recourse.

5. To prevent inaccuracy in delivery and inconvenience in the settlement of the Purchases, no Lot can, on any account, be removed during the sale.

6. If, for any cause, an article purchased cannot be delivered in as good condition as the same may have been at the time of its sale, or should any article purchased thereafter be stolen, misdelivered, or lost, the undersigned are not to be held liable in any greater amount than the price bid by the purchaser.

7. Upon failure to comply with the above conditions, the money deposited in part payment shall be forfeited; all Lots uncleared within the time aforesaid shall be re-sold by public or private Sale, without further notice, and the deficiency (if any) attending such re-sale, shall be made good by the defaulter at this Sale, together with all charges attending the same. This Condition is without prejudice to the right of the Auctioneer to enforce the contract made at this Sale, without such re-sale, if he thinks fit.

ORTGIFS & CO.,
MANAGERS.

ROBERT SOMERVILLE,
AUCTIONEER.

Catalogue

Wednesday Evening, December 7th

The first number of the size indicates
the width of the picture

I

ENRIQUEZ (J.)   .   .   .   .   Paris

The Rendezvous

2½ x 4

2

UNKNOWN

Reception to Lafayette

4 x 3

Water Color

3

ELDER (John A.)   .   .   Richmond

Landscape

3

UNKNOWN

Moonlight

$3\frac{1}{2} \times 2\frac{1}{2}$

5

ST. CENYS   .   .   Paris

French Village

$12\frac{1}{2} \times 8\frac{1}{2}$

6

RUDELL (P. E.)   .   .   New York

Landscape

$15\frac{1}{2} \times 12$

7

BISHOP (B)   .   .   New York

Trout

8×16

WARE (J.) . . Boston

Scene in Brittany

10 x 13½

9

PERKINS (Granville) . . New York

Twilight, New York Harbor

14½ x 9½

10

UNKNOWN

Flemish Scene

Water Color

11

UNKNOWN

Charles First of England

5 x 7

12

NEHLIG (Victor), N. A.   .   New York

Time of the Crusades

$11\frac{1}{2} \times 7\frac{1}{2}$

13

RUDELL (P. E.)   .   .   .   New York

Landscape

14 X 17

14

BRIDGES (Fidelia), A. N. A. . Connecticut

Robin Redbreast

6 x 7

Water Color

15

BRIDGES (Fidelia), A. N. A. . Connecticut

Robin Redbreast

$6 \times 7\frac{1}{2}$

Water Color

KOST (Fred) . . . . New York

Winter Twilight

$12\frac{1}{2} \times 7$

VALLEE (E. Max) . . . . Paris

La Gardeuse d'Oise

17×12

.

CULVER (L. B.) . . . New York

In the Woods

$14 \times 9\frac{1}{2}$

DEBUEL (Laurent) . . . Hague

Landscape and Goats

$9\frac{1}{2} \times 7$

20

DOLPH (J. H.), A. N. A.   New York

Monk

5½ x 6½

21

EHINGER

Landscape

10 x 4½

Water Color

22

BERNHARDT (Sarah)   .   Paris

The Parisienne

7 x 10

With Autograph

23

CAPELLO (A. G.)   .   .   .   Montreal

The Plains of the West

10 x 6½

24

CRAIG (Thomas)   .   New York

Turning the Fallow

34½ x 18½

25

LEWIS (H.)   .   Dusseldorf

Farm Yard

10 x 14

26

VIDAL (Vincent)   .   .   Paris

Pupil of Delaroche.
Medals, 1844-1849.
Legion of Honor, 1852.

Girl's Head

8 x 10

Water Color

27

RUDELL (P. E.)   New York

Landscape

19 x 11

9

PIETTE (L.)

French Country House

$8 \times 5\frac{1}{2}$

Water Color

DIELMAN (F.), N. A. . New York

Madison Square at Night

$7\frac{1}{2} \times 9\frac{1}{2}$

OESTY (A.) . . . , Paris

The Brunette

$14\frac{1}{2} \times 17\frac{1}{2}$

VERNON (P.) . . Paris

Landscape

$13 \times 9\frac{1}{2}$

PERRY (E. Wood), N. A.   New York

The Spinning Wheel

11½ x 14

FULLER (R. H.)   .   . Boston

Near Chelsea, Mass.

11½ x 7½

MORGAN (William), A. N. A.   . New York

Female Head

15 x 19½

BLAKELOCK (R. A.)   New York

Landscape

12 x 8

RUDELL (P. E.) . . New York

Sunset

$17\frac{1}{2}$ x $11\frac{1}{2}$

PROTAIS (Paul A.) . . . Paris

Pupil of Desmoulins.
Medals, 1863, 1864, 1865, 1878.
Legion of Honor, 1865.
Office of the Legion of Honor, 1877.

Soldier

8 x 10

Water Color

TADEMA (Mrs. Alma) . . London

Out of Work

7 x 10

DOLPH (J. H.), A. N. A. . New York

Hackensack Valley

$13\frac{1}{2}$ x $7\frac{1}{2}$

TAIT (A. F.), N. A. . . New York

Quail and Young

12 x 9

BAKER (Geo. A.), N. A., dec'd . New York

Pupil Academy of Design.
Born, 1821. Died, 1880.

"Faith"

7 x 9

WIGGINS (Carleton), A. N. A. . New York

Cows at the Pool

12 x 15

DESHAYS (E.) . . . Paris

Landscape

17½ x 9

44

BRISSOT DE WARVILLE . Paris

Pupil of Cogniet.
Medal, 1882.
Hors Concours.

Landscape and Sheep

9 x 6

45

RUDELL (P. E.) . . . New York

Landscape

$15\frac{1}{2}$ x $11\frac{1}{2}$

46

UNKNOWN

Belgian Scene

10 x 7

47

HART (Jas. M.), N. A. . . New York

Landscape

16 x 10

ROSIERSE (T.) . Brussels

The Storm

14 x 19

BAIRD (Wm.) . . Paris

Pupil of Yvon.

Scene in Brittany

13 x 9

PLASSAN (A. E.) . . . Paris

Medals, 1852, 1857, 1859.
Legion of Honor, 1859.
Medal, Philadelphia, 1876.

Baby's Toilet

5 x 6$^1_2$

IRVING (J. B.), N. A., dec'd

In the Cathedral

8 x 9$^1_2$

52

CASILEAR (J. W.), N. A.   New York

Landscape

16 x 8½

53

RUDELL (P. E.)   .   .   .   New York

Autumn

17½ x 13½

54

LEUTZE (E.), N. A., dec'd

Queen Elizabeth and Sir Walter Raleigh

63 x 47

55

BELLOWS (A. F.), N. A., dec'd

Winter

5½ x 7½

BELLOWS (A. F.), N. A., dec'd

Pool in the Woods

$5\frac{1}{2} \times 7\frac{1}{2}$

JONES (Bolton), N. A. . New York

View of Tangiers

21 X 11

PEELE (John T.) . . . London

Member of the Society of British Artists.

A Primrose Bank

29 x 24

BRISSOT DE WARVILLE (Felix) Paris

Pupil of Cogniet.
Medal, Paris, 1882.
Hors Concours.

Landscape and Sheep

25 X 21

BAZIN (Charles L.), dec'd   .   .   Paris

Pupil of Gérard.
Medals, 1844-46.
Born, 1802. Died, 1859.

The Friends

25 x 31

ANDRIOTTI

The Amateur

$15\frac{1}{2}$ x $11\frac{1}{2}$

RICHARDS (W. T.), N. A.   .   Philadelphia

Break, Break, Break

13 x 15

Water Color

PELOUSE (Louis Germain)   .   .   Paris

Born at Pierrelaye.
Medals, Paris, 1873, 1876, 1878.
Legion of Honor, 1878.

The River Bank

21 x $14\frac{1}{2}$

RIBERA (School of)

St. Peter

28 x 34

RUDELL (P. E.)   .   .   .   New York

Landscape

23 x 15½

BRANCACCIO (C.)   .   .   .   Naples

Pupil of Ziem.
Member of the Fine Arts Academy, Naples and Florence
Gold Medal, Venice, 1878; Turin, 1882.

Landscape

23 x 10

REAM (Morston)   .   .   .   New York

Fruit, Wine and Flowers

10 x 11½

ACHENBACH (Oswald)　　.　　Dusseldorf

Pupil of his brother.
Medals, 1859, 1861, 1863.
Legion of Honor, 1863.

𝕷𝖆𝖓𝖉𝖘𝖈𝖆𝖕𝖊

13½ x 10½

69

FLEURY (Francois), dec'd　　.　　Paris'

Medals, Paris, 1837, 1841, 1845.
Legion of Honor, 1851.

𝕱𝖊𝖒𝖆𝖑𝖊 𝕳𝖊𝖆𝖉

10 x 13

70

WHITTREDGE (Worthington), N. A.
New York

𝕷𝖆𝖐𝖊 𝕲𝖊𝖔𝖗𝖌𝖊

24 x 12

71

BLACKMAN (Walter)　.　.　New York

Pupil of Gérôme.

𝕍𝖊𝖓𝖎𝖈𝖊

9 x 13½

RUDELL (P. E.) . New York

Landscape

27½ x 17

COLMAN (Sam'l), N. A. . New York

Near Greenwich, Conn.

17 x 9

Water Color

JIMINEZ (Luis) . , . Paris

Pupil of Seville Academy.
Medal, 1837.
Grand Prize, Universal Exhibition, 1839.
Legion of Honor, 1839.

In the Studio

7½ x 11

GAY (Edward), A. N. A. New York

A Quiet Day

12½ x 14½

WINDMAIER (H.)

Moonlight

45 x 21½

77

ROY (Marius) . . . Lyons

Medal, Paris, 189?.

News from Home

16½ x 10

78

HASBROUCK (D. F.) . . New York

Winter Evening

12 x 9½

79

RUDELL (P. E.) . . . New York

Edge of the Village

29½ x 22

PEOTROWSKI (A.) . . . Paris

The Advanced Guard

36 x 21

MOUCHOT (L.) . . . . Paris

Medals, Paris, 1865, 1867, 1868.
Legion of Honor, 1872.

In the Refectory

28 x 23

Thursday Evening, December 8th

82

WARE (J.) . . . . . Boston

Brittany Landscape

13 x 8½

83

FULLER (R. H.) . . . Boston

Landscape

12 x 7½

84

CULVER (L. B.) . . . New York

A Relic of the Last Century

14½ x 19½

85

EYTINGE (Sol.) . . New York

Stiggins and Mrs. Weller

11½ x 9½

24

86

DEBUEL (Laurent   Hague

Landscape and Sheep

9½ x 7

87

BELLOWS (A. F.), N. A., dec'd

At the Ford

6 x 7½

88

ELDER (John A.)   .   .   Richmond

Scene in West Virginia

15 x 11½

89

TURNER (R.)   New York

Off Fortress Monroe

17½ x 11½

90

SONNTAG (W. L.), N. A.   New York

Landscape

19½ x 14

91

DARLEY (F. O. C.), N. A., dec'd

Wild Horses

18 x 9½

India Drawing

92

RUDELL (P. E.)   .   .   New York

Landscape

16½ x 13

93

LEWIS (H.   .   .   Dusseldorf

Moonlight on the Rhine

16 x 11

RICCI (Pio) . . Rome

A Love Letter

8 x 13½

SHEPPARD (W. L.) . Richmond

Sir Thomas More's Daughter

7 x 12

Black and White

TEN KATE (M.) . . Paris

Resting

13½ x 9½

Water Color

BELLOWS (A. F., N. A., dec'd

Haying

5½ x 7½

BELLOWS A. F., N. A., dec'd

November

$5\frac{1}{2} \times 7\frac{1}{2}$

99

RUDELL (P. E.) .   New York

Evening Landscape

100

TOFANO (E.) . . . . Paris

Pupil of Morelli.

At the Window

6 x 10

Water Color

101

BRISSOT DE WARVILLE . . Paris

Pupil of Cogniet.
Medal, 1873.
Hors Concours.

Landscape and Sheep

8 x 5

PEALE (Rembrandt), dec'd

John Randolph of Roanoke

2½ x 3

Miniature

DOLPH (J. H.), A. N. A.   .   New York

Monk

5½ x 6½

HOEBER (Arthur)   .   .   New York

Pupil of Gérôme.

Twilight

21½ x 12½

HASBROUCK (D. F.),   .   .   New York

A Frosty Morning

35½ x 21½

HERRICK (Mrs. S. Bledsoe)

A Corner in the Studio

21½ x 27

RUDELL (P. E.) . . . New York

Landscape

19½ x 11

KOST (Fred) . . . . New York

The Last Gleam

12 x 7

COUTOURIER (P. L.) . Paris

Pupil of Picot.
Medals, 1855, 1861.

Barnyard Friends

22 x 16

RICO (M.)   .   .   Paris

Pupil of Madrazo.
Medal, 1878.
Legion of Honor, 1878.
Medal, Universal Exhibition, 1889.

Italian Alps

20 x 14

Water Color

111

BEYSCHLAG (J. R.)   .   . Munich

Pupil of Munich Academy.

Lovers

21 x 27

112

BAIRD (Wm.)   .   .   Paris

Pupil of Yvon.

On the Seine

$17\frac{1}{2}$ x $12\frac{1}{2}$

VERNON (Paul) . . Paris

Landscape

13½ x 10

DESHAYES (E.) . . . . Paris

Holland Landscape

8 x 9

Water Color

PELHAM (J.) . . . . Paris

French Country Road

11 x 6½

Water Color

PERRY (E. Wood), N. A. . New York

The Red Ear

11½ x 14

BROWN (J. G.), N. A.   .   New York

Springtime

8 x 11½

RUDELL (P. E.)   .   .   .   New York

Driving Home the Flock

14½ x 11

BRELING (H.)   .   .   .   Munich

Rest by the Road

7 x 5

BEAUQUESNE (W. C.)   .   .   Paris

Born a Rennes.
Medals, Paris, 1875 and 1880.
Legion of Honor, 1878.
Chevalier of the Order of Leopold.

In the Guard Room

31 x 25

ROSSI (L.)   Paris

The Connoisseur

7½ x 10

Water Color

AUBERT (Jean) . . . . Paris

Pupil of Delaroche.
Medals, 1861, 1878, 1889.
Legion of Honor, 1889.

Girl's Head

13 x 16

RUDELL (P. E.) . . . New York

Landscape

19 x 15½

SEIGNAC (P.) . . . . Paris

Pupil of Frère.
Honorable Mention, 1889.

A French Wedding at Ecouën

30½ x 22½

SMITH (Henry P.) . . New York

Old Whitby, England

12 x 15

126

LAMBINET (E.), dec'd : . Paris

Pupil of Drolling.
Medals, 1843, 1853, 1857.
Legion of Honor, 1867.
Born, 1810. Died, 1878.

Landscape

15½ x 8½

127

COLEMAN (S.), N. A. . New York

Street in Grenada

12 x 15

128

VEDDER (E.), N. A. . . Rome

On the Beach

7½ x 4½

RUDELL (P. E.)　　.　　.　　. 　New York
Early Autumn
26 x 18½

BAUGNIET (Chas.), dec'd　　.　　.　　Paris

Pupil of Willems.
Chevalier of the Order of Leopold, 1843.
Officer of the same, 1872.
Member of the Order of Isabella the Catholic, the Branche Ernestine of
Saxony and Christ of Portugal.
Born, 1814.　Died, 1886.

Sympathy
10½ x 12½
Water Color

131

BROWN (J. Appleton)　　.　　.　　New York
Apple Blossoms
20½ x 16½

132

INNESS (George), N. A.　　.　　New York
Near Englewood, N. J.
17½ x 11½

RITTER (Caspar)   .   Munich

Waiting

$21\frac{1}{2}$ x $26\frac{1}{2}$

RICHARDS (Wm. T.)   .   Newport

Medal, Centennial Exhibition, 1876.
Prize Medal, Penn. Academy of Fine Arts, 1885.
Honorary Member National Academy, N. Y.

A Sandy Shore

27 x $16\frac{1}{2}$

Water Color

LINDERUM (R.)   .   Munich

A Good Tune

$11\frac{1}{2}$ x $15\frac{1}{2}$

BARGUE (Charles), dec'd   .   Paris

Painter and Model

7 x 9

Water Color

RUDELL (P. E.)   New York

𝕷𝖆𝖓𝖉𝖘𝖈𝖆𝖕𝖊

$24\frac{1}{2}$ x $17\frac{1}{2}$

138

BRILLOUIN (Louis Georges)   Paris

Pupil of Drölling and Cabat.
Medals, Paris, 1865, 1869, 1874.

𝕿𝖍𝖊 𝕯𝖎𝖘𝖈𝖔𝖗𝖉𝖆𝖓𝖙 𝕹𝖔𝖙𝖊

$14\frac{1}{2}$ x 18

139

KOEK-KOEK (B. C.), dec'd . Amsterdam

Pupil of Schelfont.
Member of the Rotterdam and St. Petersburg Academies.
Member of the Order of the Lion of the Netherlands and Leopold of
Belgium.
Medals at Amsterdam and The Hague.
Medals, Paris, 1840, 1843.
Born, 1803. Died, 1862.

𝕺𝖓 𝖙𝖍𝖊 𝕽𝖔𝖆𝖉 𝖙𝖔 𝕸𝖆𝖗𝖐𝖊𝖙

10 x 8

Water Color

CHARNAY (A.) . . . . Paris

Pupil of Pils.
Medals, 1876, 1886, 1889.

In the Garden

$9\frac{3}{4}$ x $12\frac{3}{4}$

LENOIR (P. L.), dec'd . . . Paris

Pupil of Gérôme.
Medal, 1876.
Born, 1850. Died, 1881.

A Love Token

20 x 29

JIMINEZ (Luis) . . . Paris

Pupil of Seville Academy.
Medal, 1887.
Grand Prize, Universal Exhibition, 1889.
Legion of Honor, 1889.

Awaiting an Audience

4 x $5\frac{1}{2}$

143

TOULMOUCHE (A.)   Paris

Pupil of Gleyre.
Medals, 1852, 1859, 1861, 1873.
Legion of Honor, 1870.

Memories

9 x 15

144

RUDELL (P. E.) . . .   New York

Landscape

28 x 23

145

KRAY (W.)   . . . .   Vienna

Professor of Academy at Vienna.

Psyche

30 x 42½

146

WIGGINS (Carleton), A. N. A. . New York

The Road to Montcour

16 x 20

40

GOUBIE (Jean R.) . . . Paris

Pupil of Gérôme
Medal, 1874.
Medal, Universal Exhibition, 1889.

Off for the Races

5 x 3

Water Color

DAUBIGNY (C. F.), dec'd . . Paris

Pupil of Delaroche.
Medals, 1848, 1853, 1855, 1857, 1859, 1857.
Legion of Honor, 1859.
Officer of the Legion of Honor, 1874.
Diploma to the memory of deceased artists, Universal Exhibition, 1878.
Born, 1817. Died, 1873.

Landscape

14 x 7

TAMBURINI (A.) . . . Rome

Medals in Florence and Rome.

Waiting for the Barber

10 x 12

RUDELL (P. E. . . . . New York

Road by the Riverside

$27\frac{1}{2}$ x $17\frac{1}{2}$

WOOD (Ogden) . . . Paris

Pupil of Van Marcke.

Black and White Cow

24 x 18

MORAN (Thos.), N. A. . . New York

The Rapids, Niagara Falls

$29\frac{1}{2}$ x $19\frac{1}{2}$

BODDIEN (G. von) . . Berlin

The Attack

$36\frac{1}{2}$ x 30

RUDELL (P. E.) . New York

September Landscape

35½ x 19½

GUILLEMIN (A. M.), dec'd . . Paris

Pupil of Gros.
Medals, 1841, 1845.
Legion of Honor, 1861.
Born, 1817. Died, 1880.

A Print Seller

16 x 12

LEUTZE (Emanuel), dec'd . New York

Pupil of Lessing.
Born, 1816. Died, 1863.

Henry VIII. and Anne Boleyn

16 x 28

BOLDINI (J.) . . . . Paris

Grand Prize, Universal Exhibition, 1889.

Jealousy

4½ x 6½

BISSCHOP (Christophe   Amsterdam

Pupil of Gleyre.
Medals, Philadelphia, 1876; Paris, 1878; Universal Exhibition, 1889.

The Goose Girl

18 x 22

THOMPSON (Wordsworth), N. A.
New York

Virginia in Revolutionary Times

34^{1}_{2} x 24

GIFFORD (S. R.), N. A., dec'd

Indian Summer on the Hudson

14 x 7

WEBER (Otto), dec'd   .   .   .   Berlin

Pupil of Couture.
Medals, 1864, 1869.
Born ——. Died, 1875.

Scene in Brittany

36 x 25

HUBNER (Carl), dec'd . . Dusseldorf

**Pupil of Sohn.
Chevalier of the Order of Leopold.
Medal at Metz.
Royal Professor at Dusseldorf.
Member of the Amsterdam Academy.
Born, 1814. Died, 1879.**

Emigrant's Farewell

40 x 30

.

163

BEARD (Wm. H.), N. A. . New York

Bears on a Bender

60 x 40

ORTGIES & CO.,
MANAGERS.

ROBERT SOMERVILLE,
AUCTIONEER.

www.ingramcontent.com/pod-product-compliance
Lightning Source LLC
Chambersburg PA
CBHW021557270326
41931CB00009B/1268